What Is the Story of Captain Picard?

by David Stabler

illustrated by Robert Squier

Penguin Workshop

For my father—DS

For Dan S., a generally peaceful,
sentient humanoid life form—RS

PENGUIN WORKSHOP
An imprint of Penguin Random House LLC, New York

First published in the United States of America by Penguin Workshop,
an imprint of Penguin Random House LLC, New York, 2023

Visit us online at penguinrandomhouse.com.

Library of Congress Cataloging-in-Publication Data is available.

Printed in the United States of America

ISBN 9781524791179 (paperback)   10 9 8 7 6 5 4 3 2 1 WOR
ISBN 9781524791186 (library binding)   10 9 8 7 6 5 4 3 2 1 WOR

Contents

Jean-Luc Picard

What Is the Story of Captain Picard?

On the evening of September 28, 1987, *Star Trek* fans all over the world turned on their TV sets with great anticipation. For the first time in thirteen years, a new episode of their favorite series would be airing. But this time the show would be different. *Star Trek: The Next Generation* had a new look, a new cast . . . and a new captain in command of the *U.S.S. Enterprise*-D. Trek fans were about to meet Jean-Luc Picard.

The first episode, "Encounter at Farpoint," showed the new crew being assembled and sent to solve a mystery at the Farpoint space station. Along the way, they encounter "Q," an all-powerful alien who takes an intense interest in the ship's freshly installed commander.

By the end of the two-hour premiere episode, Picard would solve the mystery of Farpoint, outwit Q, and earn the respect of his new crew. The *Enterprise*, it seemed, was in good hands.

In many ways, "Encounter at Farpoint" was a typical *Star Trek* episode. It featured strange aliens, dangerous situations, and plenty of science fiction intrigue. Captain Picard opened the show with the words "Space, the final frontier . . ." just as the original *Enterprise* captain, James T. Kirk, had back in the 1960s when the original *Star Trek* series aired on television. Dr. Leonard McCoy, the ship's surgeon on that show, even dropped by for a visit. But much had changed as well. There were more women officers on the ship. Many of the crewmembers had family—including small children—with them on board. An android, or artificial life form, sat on the bridge in place of the Vulcan science officer Mr. Spock. And Captain Picard relied on his wits more than his fists to solve problems. A bald, businesslike man of French descent, Picard is just as daring as his predecessor but with a more diplomatic flair.

Data, an android, on the bridge

It took a while for some fans to adjust to all these changes. They hoped the old *Star Trek* would return. But most viewers were willing to give the new show a chance. They trusted the man who created the show, Gene Roddenberry, and they were eager to see where he would take the new crew and its captain. As it turned out,

Star Trek: The Next Generation remained on TV for seven years. The new crewmembers became just as beloved as Captain Kirk, Mr. Spock, and Dr. McCoy. Captain Jean-Luc Picard went on to be the most popular of them all. He led his crew through four movies and even got his own spin-off series, *Star Trek: Picard*, in 2020. But you would have never predicted that on that September evening in 1987 when "Encounter at Farpoint" premiered. This is the story of Captain Picard—the man who saved *Star Trek* and became one of its biggest stars.

CHAPTER 1
The New Captain

The final episode of the original *Star Trek* series aired on the NBC network on June 3, 1969. The cast and crew moved on to other projects. For creator and producer Gene Roddenberry, it was the end of a three-year mission to bring smart science fiction to American television. Everyone thought the show was gone forever. Everyone except the fans, that is.

In the early 1970s, *Star Trek* fans began to organize themselves. They gathered at *Star Trek* conventions, which are large meetings where they could celebrate the show, dress up as favorite characters, and buy and sell books, toys, and other merchandise. Reruns of the original seventy-nine episodes on local TV stations

began to attract new fans to the show as well. Some of them asked the network to reunite the cast and bring the *Enterprise* crew back for another season.

Gene Roddenberry started to believe that his *Star Trek* dream could be revived. In 1973, he persuaded NBC to let him create a new show, *Star Trek: The Animated Series*. The cartoon version of the *Enterprise*'s adventures aired for two seasons on Saturday mornings and featured the voices of many members of the original cast. After it went off the air in 1974, Roddenberry set his sights on bringing the crew back for new live-action TV adventures. The executives at Paramount Studios were still not convinced that *Star Trek* was popular enough, though, and they rejected all of Roddenberry's ideas. It was only after the phenomenal success of the feature film *Star Wars* in 1977 that Hollywood began to reconsider.

In 1978, the Paramount movie studio announced that they had hired Gene Roddenberry to create an all-new *Star Trek* movie featuring the original crew. *Star Trek: The Motion Picture* was released in December 1979 and became a box office success. Three more *Star Trek* features followed over the next seven years.

By 1986, Gene Roddenberry was looking for a new challenge. Although he was happy with the movie series' success, he still longed to see *Star Trek* back on television where it all began. He liked the idea of starting over with a whole new captain and crew. Television executives agreed that the time was right for the "next generation" to take over.

Gene Roddenberry (1921–1991)

Eugene Wesley Roddenberry was born in El Paso, Texas. His family moved to Los Angeles, California, when he was still a baby. As a young man, he worked as a pilot and a police officer before becoming a writer and producer for television.

In the early 1960s, Roddenberry wrote for several successful TV shows. He specialized in Westerns and police dramas. But he left his biggest mark in science fiction. He is the writer, creator, and producer of the original series *Star Trek*, which first appeared on television in 1966.

After *Star Trek* went off the air in 1969, Roddenberry began to travel across the United States to meet fans of the show at the first *Star Trek* conventions. He became known by the nickname "The Great Bird of the Galaxy." He even started his own company selling toys, games, and other *Star Trek* products. But his fondest wish was to see *Star Trek* return, either as a TV series or a movie. And he saw both those wishes come true.

Gene Roddenberry died in 1991, as *Star Trek: The Next Generation*'s fourth season was underway. In 1994, the "Roddenberry Crater" on the planet Mars was named in his honor.

In October of that year, a new weekly *Star Trek* TV series was announced. It would begin airing in the fall of 1987. Roddenberry now had less than one year to put the show together.

He started by assembling an all-star team of writers and producers to help him bring his

vision to life. Over the next few months, they assembled a list of characters for the new series. Topping that list was the *Enterprise*'s new captain, Jean-Luc Picard. Roddenberry picked that name to honor two Swiss scientists he admired, twin brothers Auguste and Jean Piccard.

Roddenberry modeled Picard after one of his favorite fictional characters, Captain Horatio Hornblower. Hornblower is a nineteenth-century English sea captain in a series of books written by C. S. Forester. He is known for his intelligence but also for being uncomfortable around other people. Roddenberry instructed his writers to keep these traits in mind when writing for the character of Captain Picard. He also told them the next *Enterprise* commander had to be French. Many actors auditioned for the part of Jean-Luc Picard. One of them was Patrick Stewart.

Although he was a fine performer, he didn't seem to fit what Roddenberry had in mind. For one thing, he was British, not French. For another, he was as bald as an egg. He had started to lose his hair at age nineteen. Roddenberry immediately crossed Stewart off his list, but encouraged him to try out for another role, the android officer Lieutenant Commander Data. Stewart wasn't interested in playing a secondary part, however. He wanted to sit in the captain's chair.

A number of the other producers agreed. They thought Patrick Stewart was the right man for the role. Over the next several weeks, they urged Gene Roddenberry to reconsider. Eventually, he agreed to take another look at the stage actor. The producers called Stewart and asked him to come back for another meeting with Roddenberry and studio executives. They also reminded him that Gene envisioned Picard as having wavy, flowing hair.

Patrick Stewart immediately called home to London and had a special hairpiece shipped over to Hollywood for his audition. He showed up to the meeting wearing a wig! He read a scene as Picard and immediately impressed everyone in the room. Even Gene Roddenberry could see that

he was the perfect actor to play Picard. One of
the executives then rose from his chair and sealed
the deal.

"That's your guy," he told Roddenberry. Then he turned to Patrick Stewart. "But lose the wig."

Patrick Stewart (1940–)

Patrick Stewart was born in the West Yorkshire town of Mirfield, England. He began acting in grade school, after one of his teachers gave him a copy of a play by William Shakespeare. After training at the Royal Shakespeare Company, Stewart became one of his country's most accomplished stage actors.

In the 1970s, Stewart began taking on more

and more television and movie roles. He played a villainous Roman military officer on the TV miniseries *I, Claudius* and a noble king in the film *Excalibur*. After a successful run in TV and film as Jean-Luc Picard, he went on to play Professor Charles Francis Xavier (aka "Professor X") in the *X-Men* movie series between 2000 and 2017. The Marvel Universe series also gave him the chance to act opposite one of his closest friends, Ian McKellen, who played the supervillain Magneto.

In 2008, he was nominated for a Tony Award for his performance in William Shakespeare's *Macbeth* on Broadway. In 2010, in a royal ceremony, Stewart was knighted by Queen Elizabeth II. From that day forward, he would be known as Sir Patrick Stewart. And in 2016, the drama building at the University of Huddersfield, near his childhood home in England, was renamed the "Sir Patrick Stewart Building" in his honor.

CHAPTER 2
Engage!

With a new captain in place, the producers of *Star Trek: The Next Generation* began filling the other positions on the *Enterprise*. Actor Jonathan Frakes was hired to play Commander William T. Riker, Picard's loyal first officer. As Dr. Beverly Crusher, the ship's medical officer, producers

William T. Riker and Dr. Beverly Crusher

chose dancer and actress Gates McFadden. Wil Wheaton was cast as Wesley Crusher, Beverly's son, a teenage genius who repeatedly saves the ship from danger.

Wesley Crusher

Denise Crosby played Tasha Yar, the *Enterprise*'s chief of security. The tactical officer was Worf, a Klingon played by Michael Dorn.

Tasha Yar and Geordi La Forge

The Klingons had been villains on the original series, but now they were allies of the United Federation of Planets. British actress Marina Sirtis took on the role of Deanna Troi, the ship's counselor, a native of the planet Betazed who can "sense" the emotions of other beings. LeVar Burton, the host of the children's TV show

Reading Rainbow and star of the miniseries *Roots*, accepted the part of helmsman Geordi La Forge. He would later become the ship's chief engineer.

Worf and Deanna Troi

The last starring role went to veteran stage and TV actor Brent Spiner. He was cast as Lieutenant Commander Data, the part that Patrick Stewart had turned down. An android who wants to experience human feelings, Data would play the role of an outsider among the *Enterprise* crew.

Especially in the earliest episodes, he spent a lot of time misunderstanding figures of speech and doing complex equations in his head. Many viewers likened him to Mr. Spock, the emotionless first officer from the original series. Like Spock, Data would become a fan favorite character. He would also emerge as one of Captain Picard's closest friends.

It took some time for all the actors to get to know one another. Some of them did not feel comfortable working with Patrick Stewart, because he was so serious. They played practical jokes on him to get him to loosen up. At first, Stewart did not take kindly to these pranks. But over time he grew more at ease with his fellow cast members.

In the early episodes of *Star Trek: The Next Generation*, you can see that Jean-Luc Picard is a lot like Patrick Stewart. During the first season of *TNG*, Captain Picard is all business.

Meet the Captains

Jean-Luc Picard was not the first to command a starship named *Enterprise*. Here are some of the courageous commanders who came before him.

Jonathan Archer was the commanding officer of the first starship *Enterprise*. A true pioneer with a thirst for adventure (and a pet beagle named Porthos), he is considered the greatest explorer of the twenty-second century. He is played by actor Scott Bakula on the TV series *Star Trek: Enterprise*.

Robert April appears on an episode of *Star Trek: The Animated Series*. His wife, Sarah, was the *Enterprise*'s chief medical officer during the years he was in command.

Christopher Pike, played by actor Jeffrey Hunter, commands the *Enterprise* in the original series' pilot episode, "The Cage." He is severely injured in the line of duty and appears in a mind-controlled wheelchair in the episode "The Menagerie."

James T. Kirk is the most famous of the *Enterprise* captains. Played by William Shatner in all seventy-nine episodes of the original series (and in seven movies), Kirk is a bold and brave action hero who also knows how to outwit his opponents.

James T. Kirk

Rachel Garrett appears in the classic *Next Generation* episode "Yesterday's Enterprise." She assumes command some time in the twenty-fourth century and leads the *Enterprise* on a mission to save a Klingon outpost from attack by the Romulans. She is played by actress Tricia O'Neil.

He rarely leaves the bridge of the *Enterprise*, preferring to send his first officer, Will Riker, to explore other planets in his place. And he takes his job seriously.

Captain Picard wore a close-fitting stretchy uniform that inspired one of his most famous character traits. To keep the material from bunching up on him, Patrick Stewart began tugging it down during filming. This habit became known by fans the world over as the

Picard Maneuver. Stewart kept doing it long after the uniforms were replaced two years later.

The Picard Maneuver wasn't the only signature move Picard developed during season one. He also became famous for two catchphrases. "Make it so" was something he said when giving a command or putting a plan into motion.

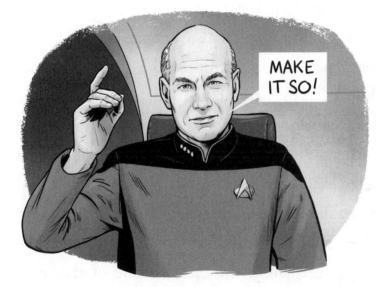

MAKE IT SO!

It's actually a very old expression used by officers in the British Navy. "Engage" was something Picard often said when instructing his helm officer to go to warp speed. While it's become one of Picard's best-known lines, he wasn't the first *Enterprise* captain to use it. In "The Cage," Captain Christopher Pike instructs his helmsman to take off by telling him to "engage." Captain James T. Kirk even says "engage" in an episode of the original series (although he usually prefers to say "Take us out, Mr. Sulu").

Captain Picard is also known for drinking a particular type of tea. In fact, he is shown sipping hot tea in the very first episode of *TNG*. But the special blend he prefers isn't mentioned until the series' thirty-sixth episode, "Contagion," which aired in the middle of the second season. "Tea, Earl Grey, hot," Picard tells the *Enterprise* replicator, the device that serves up food and drinks to the crew. Amazingly, this became one of the most famous lines of the entire series! Picard would repeat his order many times over the course of seven seasons. So what is Earl Grey tea and who is

it named for? It's a flavored black tea named after a nineteenth-century British nobleman, Charles Grey.

Season one was now complete. The new crew had been introduced, along with new and old enemies like Q, the Romulans, and the Ferengi. Viewers got to see what an all-new starship *Enterprise* could do—including the addition of a battle bridge for duels in space. Captain Picard's basic personality and unique catchphrases were in place. Now the writers and Patrick Stewart just had to fill in the details of the character. The life and times of Jean-Luc Picard were about to be written.

CHAPTER 3
Picard's Journey

Jean-Luc Picard was born in La Barre, France, on July 13, 2305. His parents, Maurice and Yvette Picard, owned a small family vineyard, which Jean-Luc and his older brother, Robert, helped

run. Growing up, Jean-Luc spoke French and learned to sing traditional French children's songs like "Frère Jacques."

Maurice Picard hoped that Jean-Luc would remain in La Barre and help manage the family vineyard one day, but Jean-Luc had other ideas. He became fascinated by the work of Starfleet, the organization created by the United Federation of Planets whose mission was to explore the universe. When he was in grade school, Jean-Luc wrote a paper about Starfleet and was awarded a ribbon for excellence.

Jean-Luc's brother, Robert, always envied his success at school. He believed that their parents favored Jean-Luc and let him get away with misbehavior that he would have been punished for. At times, Robert took out his frustrations by bullying his younger brother.

As soon as he was old enough, Jean-Luc sought to leave La Barre and escape his brother's bullying. He applied to Starfleet Academy, but was rejected. He tried again and was accepted in 2323. He left the vineyard behind and didn't return to France for many years.

At Starfleet Academy, Jean-Luc was a dedicated student, graduating at the top of his class. He took an interest in archaeology but turned down an offer from one of his professors to continue his studies in that field. While

ancient alien civilizations would always fascinate him, Jean-Luc had his sights set on becoming a Starfleet officer and serving aboard a starship.

That dream was nearly cut short when he was still an ensign in Starfleet. (Ensign is the rank just below lieutenant.) Jean-Luc was seriously injured in a fight shortly after graduation. He got into an argument with a rugged alien known as a Nausicaan and was stabbed through the heart during the struggle. Doctors had to perform emergency surgery to install an artificial heart in order to keep Jean-Luc alive.

After recovering from surgery, Ensign Picard was assigned to his first ship, the *U.S.S. Reliant*. He remained on board the *Reliant* for several years before transferring to the *U.S.S. Stargazer*, where he served as first officer. In 2333, he took command of the *Stargazer* when the captain was killed during a battle. He remained in that position for the next twenty-two years.

U.S.S. Stargazer

One of Jean-Luc's closest friends on board the *Stargazer* was Lieutenant Commander Jack Crusher. In 2353, Picard sent Jack Crusher on a hazardous away mission, where he was tragically killed. Picard had the sad task of returning Jack's body to his widow, Dr. Beverly Crusher, who would later go on to serve under him as chief medical officer on the *Enterprise*.

Jack Crusher

Aside from the tragedy of Jack Crusher's death, Picard would always look back fondly on his time aboard the *Stargazer*. But by 2364, he was ready to take on a bigger challenge: command of his own Galaxy-class starship. That year, Picard was made captain of the newly commissioned *U.S.S. Enterprise*-D, the flagship vessel of Starfleet. He looked forward to his assignment, although he was wary of getting to know a new crew—

especially on a ship with so many children on board! The prospect of reuniting with the wife of his old friend Jack Crusher also made him a little nervous. But his sense of duty soon won out.

U.S.S. Enterprise-D

He had always believed that his destiny lay among the stars. Now he was about to write the next chapter in that great adventure.

Picard's Pursuits

Jean-Luc Picard is a man of many passions. Here are some of the hobbies he likes to pursue when he's not on the bridge of the *U.S.S. Enterprise.*

Fencing. Picard is a highly skilled swordsman. He is often shown fencing, a sport that was once popular in his native France. In one famous scene from *TNG*, Picard teaches fencing to Guinan, the ship's mysterious alien bartender.

Playing music. Picard has a deep love of music and is often seen listening to classical recordings in his quarters. He plays an alien instrument known as a Ressikan flute in two famous episodes of *TNG*.

Solving mysteries. One of Picard's childhood heroes was Dixon Hill, a fictional private detective living on Earth in the early twentieth century. As an adult, Captain Picard occasionally pretends to be Dixon Hill in mystery adventures he creates on the *Enterprise*'s holodeck, a place where characters can experience a simulated environment that has been generated by the ship's computer.

Riding horses. Picard keeps a saddle in his quarters and likes nothing more than going for a ride. In the holodeck program Equestrian Adventure, he can gallop through the countryside during his off-hours aboard the *Enterprise*.

Treasure hunting. Picard loves archaeology and studying ancient alien artifacts in his spare time.

CHAPTER 4
Friends and Foes

Captain Picard is the commanding officer of the *U.S.S. Enterprise*, but he cannot run the ship on his own. He relies on his loyal crew to keep things going smoothly. Over the years,

Picard formed close friendships with a number of his fellow officers.

Commander William Thomas "Will" Riker is the *Enterprise*'s first officer and Picard's second-in-command. Picard often refers to him as "Number One" because of his high rank. According to Starfleet regulations, it is the first officer's job to keep the captain safe. Accordingly, Number One leads most of the dangerous away missions to unexplored planets.

Riker is a native of Earth. He grew up in Alaska. His mother died when he was young, and he was raised by his father, who works for Starfleet. Riker's passions include jazz music, playing the trombone, and playing poker.

He is willful and headstrong, often challenging Starfleet rules—but he never challenges the captain's authority. He has passed up several offers to command a ship of his own because he believes he still has more to learn from Captain Picard.

Picard treats Riker like a son. He encourages Riker to take command of his own ship, but never pressures him to do so. When Riker makes a mistake or runs afoul of Starfleet regulations, Captain Picard offers him support and advice. In one episode, Riker is put on trial for a crime he did not commit. Picard leads his defense and helps clear his name. Later, when Riker gets married to ship's counselor Deanna Troi, Captain Picard serves as the best man at the wedding.

Lieutenant Commander Data is another trusted member of Picard's bridge crew. Data is an android, or artificial life form. He was constructed on an alien planet by the scientist Dr. Noonian Soong. Data is the first android to attend Starfleet Academy. Although he is a highly decorated officer, he faces discrimination from some of the other crewmembers.

Data and Noonian Soong

Picard does not approve of prejudice toward androids and considers Data a valuable member of his crew. When the Starfleet scientist Dr. Bruce Maddox tries to have Data removed from the *Enterprise* in order to dismantle and "study" him, Picard comes to Data's defense. He convinces

Maddox that Data is not just a machine and has a right to say no to Maddox's request.

Over their years of service together, Data comes to rely on Picard for advice. Because Data longs to experience human emotions, Picard encourages him to paint and write poetry. Together they perform Shakespeare's plays on the holodeck. Whenever Data gives a violin recital for the crew, Picard is often in the front row leading the applause.

Data performs Shakespeare

Worf, son of Mogh, is the *Enterprise*'s chief of
security. The proud Klingon warrior saves Picard's
life on numerous occasions. To return the favor,
Picard helps Worf in his quest to clear his family
name on his home planet. When Worf needs to
return to the Klingon home world to attend to
family business, Captain Picard gives him leave
from his duties aboard the *Enterprise*. He even
travels with him and stands by his side when
Worf is put on trial before the Klingon High
Council.

Ensign Wesley Crusher is another crewmember with whom Picard has a close personal relationship. The son of his old friends Jack and Beverly Crusher, Wesley looks to Captain Picard for guidance after his father's death. Picard is uncomfortable around the teenager but feels responsible for his safety while he's on board the *Enterprise*. He encourages Wesley to attend Starfleet Academy but is disappointed when the young cadet is nearly expelled after a flying stunt turned deadly.

Finally, Picard keeps a close friendship with the *Enterprise*'s mysterious bartender, Guinan. A member of an ancient alien civilization, Guinan has known Picard for a long time—though no one knows precisely where or when they first met. Guinan is known for being a good listener and often gives Picard advice on command decisions. Picard occasionally gives Guinan fencing lessons as well.

Jean-Luc Picard has his share of enemies as well as friends. Among the villains who have squared off against him the most over the years are one old foe from the original series and three new ones created especially for *TNG*.

Cold and calculating, the Romulans sparred with Captain Kirk in the original series, and they continue to cause problems for Captain Picard in the twenty-fourth century. They are mortal enemies of the Klingons, who often come to the aid of the *Enterprise* when it has a confrontation with a Romulan vessel.

Picard deals with the Ferengi

The wily Ferengi are more like annoying pests than truly scary enemies. They return to the *Enterprise* time and time again to try to involve Picard and his crew in their moneymaking schemes. Picard usually keeps them at bay without too much trouble.

The Borg are a mysterious alien species who travel the universe in cube-shaped ships, conquering and absorbing (or, as they put it, "assimilating") the people of other worlds. The Borg kidnap Picard and force him to be their spokesperson as part of a scheme to destroy Earth.

The Borg also have major roles in the movie *Star Trek: First Contact* and the *Star Trek: Picard* series.

The Cardassians

The Cardassians are fearsome humanoid warriors who hate other races. They have been on the brink of war with the Federation for decades.

Picard must be very careful when matching wits with a Cardassian commander, for fear of breaking the peace.

And then, of course, there's Q.

Q Who?

The Q entity, often simply called Q, is Picard's oldest, most powerful foe. In the very first episode of *Star Trek: The Next Generation*, Q puts Picard on "trial" for humanity's crimes. He returns to the *Enterprise* numerous times—each time with another plan to annoy the captain. He introduces Picard to the Borg, forces the captain to play the role of Robin Hood, and transports him back in time to his days at Starfleet Academy.

Although he takes human form, Q is actually a member of a godlike alien race, the Q Continuum, that resides in another dimension. There are in fact many different Q, although the one we know best is played by actor John de Lancie. Gene Roddenberry chose the letter Q as a tribute to his friend Janet Quarton, the founder of one of the first *Star Trek* fan clubs. Q is the only villain who appears in both the first and the last episodes of *Star Trek: The Next Generation.*

CHAPTER 5
The Best of Picard

On June 18, 1990, *Star Trek: The Next Generation* fans watched in horror as the *U.S.S. Enterprise* aimed all its deadly phaser weapons on a ship containing its own captain. "Mr. Worf—fire," ordered First Officer Will Riker. Was this the end of Jean-Luc Picard? "To be continued . . ." read the words that rolled across the screen.

Viewers would have to wait three months to see the conclusion of the story, titled "The Best of Both Worlds."

The two-part epic is often ranked among the top five *TNG* episodes of all time. In part one, Picard is abducted by the villainous Borg and forced to serve as their spokesperson as they attempt to conquer planet Earth and absorb— or "assimilate"—its inhabitants into the Borg Collective. The show gave actor Patrick Stewart the chance to play two parts: the heroic Picard and his evil robotic Borg counterpart, Locutus.

Picard after being captured by the Borg

It was a challenge that Stewart had been looking forward to for a long time.

At the end of the second season of *TNG*, Stewart had lunch with Gene Roddenberry to discuss some changes he wanted to make to the character of Picard. In short, he wanted Captain

Picard to leave the ship more often, take a more active role, and maybe even go on a date from time to time. Roddenberry agreed to Stewart's suggestions, and beginning in season three, the show's writers transformed Picard from a dull and drippy diplomat into more of an action hero. "The Best of Both Worlds" was just the first of many classic Picard stories to come. (Spoiler alert: Picard survives and escapes the Borg.)

Right after his escape, Captain Picard decides to return to Earth to visit his family. In that episode, we learn all about his childhood and his rivalry with his brother, Robert. Picard is even offered a chance to give up command of the *Enterprise* and remain on Earth to work as an underwater scientist. In the end, he declines the offer. The episode, "Family," is considered another one of Picard's "greatest hits."

In June 1992, an important episode called "The Inner Light" aired. In what many Trek fans consider the greatest *Star Trek* episode of all time, Captain Picard wakes up on another planet with a different name, a wife, and a whole new identity! He lives out an entire second life with his new family before being whisked back to the *Enterprise*. The touching story won numerous awards. Patrick Stewart has ranked it as his favorite episode of the entire series. He even got to act alongside his real-life son, Daniel Stewart, who played his "son" on the show.

Patrick Stewart and Daniel Stewart in "The Inner Light"

In "Family" and "The Inner Light," Picard is tempted to give up his duties as captain of the *Enterprise* for a quiet life in the countryside.

A Very Expensive Whistle

In the classic *Star Trek: The Next Generation* episode "The Inner Light," Captain Picard learns to play a small tin whistle known as a Ressikan flute.

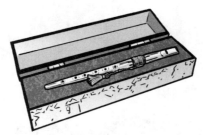

According to Patrick Stewart, the prop flute used in the show did not actually make a sound, but he did take lessons from a real-life flute player to make it *look* as if he was actually playing.

Because the episode is so beloved by *Star Trek* fans, the Ressikan flute that was used as a prop in this episode became a prized collector's item. In fact, in 2006, it was sold at an auction in New York for $48,000!

In another classic episode of *TNG*, his sense of duty is tested in another way. In "Chain of Command," Starfleet sends Picard on a top secret mission to find out about a secret Cardassian weapon. But he is taken prisoner and tortured by a Cardassian commander. The captain must summon up all his courage to keep from revealing Federation secrets to the enemy. Many *TNG* fans consider "Chain of Command" to be Patrick Stewart's finest performance as Captain Picard.

There is another episode of *The Next Generation* that makes most fans' lists of the Best of Picard. "Tapestry" tells the story of the *Enterprise* captain's early days with Starfleet. The all-powerful Q transforms Picard into his younger self and lets him correct all the mistakes Jean-Luc made as a hotheaded Starfleet cadet. He even relives the fight with the alien who nearly killed him—and caused him to need an artificial heart. In the end, Picard realizes he doesn't want to change his past. He is satisfied with the life he has, as captain of the *Enterprise*.

Each of these classic *TNG* episodes shows a different side of the personality of Jean-Luc Picard. They are all often ranked in the top ten among all 178 episodes of the series. A man of

honor and duty who sometimes wishes he could lead a quieter life with a family of his own, Picard seems very different from the brash and outspoken Captain James T. Kirk. But he is every bit as much a hero.

CHAPTER 6
All Good Things...

By the fall of 1992, *Star Trek: The Next Generation* had been on the air for five years. But for the first time, the show began a new television season without its creator. Gene Roddenberry had passed away the previous October. His loyal crew of writers and producers carried on in his absence. The show would go on—but it would not be the same without him.

Ratings for the final two seasons of *TNG* remained high. Captain Picard faced many new challenges in the seventh and final season. In one memorable episode, a strange disease transforms the entire crew of the *Enterprise* into prehistoric animals and insects. Picard himself begins changing into a tiny monkey—though he is cured before he completes his transformation.

Lieutenant Reginald Barclay turns into a spider

In another episode, a space pirate ship captures Captain Picard and makes him part of its crew. For a while, Picard even plays along in order to find out what the pirates are up to. He gets into a fight with Riker and pretends to lead an attack on the *Enterprise*. The lighthearted two-part show gave Patrick Stewart a chance to play the villain for a change, something he always enjoyed.

As the season wound down, it become clear that season seven would be *TNG*'s last. Plans were finalized for a *Next Gen* movie to begin filming immediately after the season ended. With that

in mind, the show's writers begin to think about how they wanted to wrap up the series. In the end, they decided to go out with a bang—a big bang.

"All Good Things . . . ," the last episode of *Star Trek: The Next Generation*, first aired on May 23, 1994. It was more than twice as long as a typical episode. Not surprisingly, the show's creators made the last installment a showcase for Captain Picard. It is also the final *TNG* appearance of Q, Picard's oldest and most persistent enemy.

In the episode, Picard finds himself traveling back and forth in time. He gets to relive his earliest days on the *Enterprise* and sees what life will be like for him when he is an old man.

In the end, Q reveals that he is responsible for all this—and that the trial of humanity that began in the show's first episode never really ended. The show became famous for its final scene, where Captain Picard at long last joins the officers' weekly poker game. "I should have done this a long time ago," Picard says, to the delight of his crewmembers.

The closing moment brought tears to the eyes of many of the show's loyal fans. Some viewers have even called "All Good Things . . ." the greatest final episode in TV history.

The people who vote for the Hugo Awards, the annual prizes given to the world's best science fiction, seemed to agree. They gave "All Good Things . . ." the 1995 Hugo Award for Best Dramatic Presentation. *Star Trek: The Next Generation* was also

Hugo Award

nominated for an Emmy Award for Outstanding Drama Series for the overall excellence of its final season. Most important of all, the last episode was the highest-rated episode that season—and the highest rated since the very first one, "Encounter at Farpoint," seven years earlier.

Some of the actors on *TNG* were disappointed that the series had come to an end. They believed there were many more good stories to tell. But the show's producers were now eager to tell those stories for movie audiences. They also felt it was time to make way for two new *Star Trek* television series: *Star Trek: Deep Space Nine*, which debuted in 1993, and *Star Trek: Voyager*, which was scheduled to launch in January 1995.

Just four days after Patrick Stewart and his costars finished filming the TV finale, they began working on the first of four *Star Trek: The Next Generation* movies. That project would bring Stewart face to face with his predecessor in the *Enterprise* captain's chair—and begin a new chapter in the saga of Jean-Luc Picard.

Meet More Captains

In 1987, Patrick Stewart was considered an unconventional choice to play Jean-Luc Picard. But the captains who came after him on other *Star Trek* TV series were trailblazers in their own right.

Benjamin Sisko, played by Avery Brooks, is the commanding officer of space station Deep Space Nine on *Star Trek: Deep Space Nine*, which aired from 1993 to 1999. The son of a Creole chef from New Orleans, Louisiana, Sisko is a man of many interests, including cooking, baseball, and collecting model starships. He is the first Black man to be the lead character on a *Star Trek* television series.

Kathryn Janeway, played by Kate Mulgrew from 1995 to 2001, is the captain of the *U.S.S. Voyager* on *Star Trek: Voyager*. Although there had long been female starship captains and admirals in Starfleet ranks, tough Captain Janeway was the first female captain to lead a *Star Trek* television series.

Michael Burnham, played by Sonequa Martin-Green, is the captain of the *U.S.S. Discovery* on *Star Trek: Discovery*, which launched in 2017. She is the first Black woman to be the central character on a *Star Trek* television series. A native of Earth, Burnham was raised on Vulcan by Ambassador Sarek and Amanda Grayson—the parents of Mr. Spock.

Michael Burnham

CHAPTER 7
Action Picard

The spring of 1994 was a hectic time for the cast of *Star Trek: The Next Generation*. Instead of taking a vacation, they went straight from filming the TV series to working on their first feature film together.

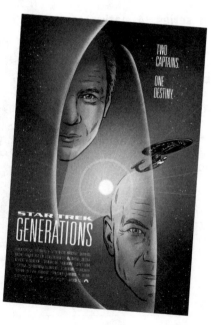

Captain Jean-Luc Picard and Captain James T. Kirk

Was it worth it? To fans who loved both the original series and *Next Gen*, it was. *Star Trek Generations* was released to movie theaters on November 18, 1994, attracting large crowds. In the movie, Picard joins forces with Captain James T. Kirk to prevent a mad scientist named Soran from destroying a solar system.

Soran

The "meeting of the minds" between *Star Trek*'s two most popular captains was only one surprise awaiting moviegoers. In the film's dramatic ending scene, Kirk and Soran get into a fistfight on a sky-high catwalk (a narrow walkway). Kirk gets the better of the supervillain and stops him from launching his star-destroying rocket. In the process, however, Kirk is thrown off the catwalk onto the desert rocks below. Picard is by his side when Kirk dies, reassuring him that his sacrifice helped save the galaxy.

It was the kind of heroic ending that Captain Kirk deserved, but it wasn't the ending originally planned. The scene was originally filmed with Soran blasting Kirk from behind with a phaser. But the first audiences who saw the film didn't like seeing the beloved Captain Kirk killed by Soran. So cast and crew returned to the desert to reshoot the scene at a cost of $4 million.

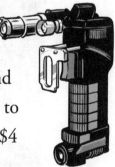

Soran's phaser

With one successful movie complete, the *Next Gen* cast finally took some well-deserved time off. But it wasn't too long before *Star Trek* producers came calling again. They proposed a second film featuring just the *Next Generation* cast. Patrick Stewart was eager to have Picard be more of the center of attention this time around and do more action scenes.

When *Star Trek: First Contact* was released in the fall of 1996, Patrick Stewart got his wish.

The movie tells the story of Captain Picard and his battle with the evil Borg queen, who has a plan to conquer Earth by changing its past.

Picard does less talking and more fighting than in the previous picture, which pleased the actor—and many fans as well. Directed by *Next Gen*'s beloved Number One, Jonathan Frakes, *First Contact* was an even bigger success than *Generations*.

It was nominated for dozens of awards, including an Academy Award for Best Makeup. Many fans consider it the best movie of the entire *Star Trek* series.

Jonathan Frakes directs *Star Trek: First Contact*

After *First Contact* earned more than $146 million worldwide, there was little doubt there would be a third *Next Gen* movie. Released in 1998, *Star Trek: Insurrection* continues the story of the *Enterprise* crew, with a few new twists. This time, Data has a malfunction that causes him to go berserk and take a group of Federation officials hostage. The *Enterprise* rushes to the scene so that Picard can deal with the crisis. There is more humor and less drama in this film than in the previous two. Captain Picard is still at the center of the story, but this time he is in love with Anij, a member of an alien people known as the Ba'ku.

Audiences seemed to like the new direction. *Insurrection* was nominated for several awards and earned more money than many of the *Star Trek* movies that came before it. Nevertheless, it would be four long years before the next film in the series.

Star Trek Nemesis was released in December 2002. The film featured a new villain, Shinzon—an evil clone of Captain Picard! When crewmembers discover a break-in on the *Enterprise* computer, they are forced into a life-or-death battle with Shinzon before he can destroy Earth. Like *Insurrection*, *Nemesis* was a departure from *Star Trek* movies that had come before. In one startling scene, set on a desert planet, Picard roars out of the back of a shuttlecraft driving a futuristic dune buggy, wearing goggles as he wheels around the desert sand.

Some fans were surprised with the *Enterprise* captain's transformation into "Action Picard."

Some were also disappointed to see the death of fan favorite character Lieutenant Commander Data. *Star Trek Nemesis* was not as successful as the previous films in the series. Plans for another movie in *The Next Generation* saga were canceled. It looked like Captain Picard's frantic dune buggy race might be his last ride.

CHAPTER 8
The Next Frontier

On January 13, 2020, a Hollywood premiere for the new CBS All Access series *Star Trek: Picard* drew a crowd of hundreds to the ArcLight Cinerama Dome. Joining series star Patrick Stewart on the red carpet were several of his *Star Trek: The Next Generation* costars. It was like a family reunion.

Viewers didn't know it yet, but some of those same costars would be appearing in episodes of *Picard* as their *TNG* characters. So how did this all-new, all-star *Star Trek* adventure come together? In 2018, the producers of the new *Star Trek: Discovery* TV series approached Patrick Stewart with an idea for an additional series centered around Jean-Luc Picard. This was not going to be a repeat of what he had done before, but a totally fresh story that would surprise even the biggest *Star Trek* fans. Plus the name "Picard" was going to be right there in the title. What's not to love?

When Patrick Stewart announced his participation to the audience at the annual Las Vegas *Star Trek* convention that August, the crowd went wild. It had been sixteen years since the last *Next Gen* movie, but now, at long last, Captain Picard was back. Retired Admiral Picard, that is. Sometime after the events of

Star Trek Nemesis, the *Enterprise*'s beloved commander had been promoted to the top ranks of Starfleet.

Star Trek: Picard premiered on January 23, 2020. The new show was set twenty years after the events of *Star Trek Nemesis*. Picard is now ninety-four years old and living on his family vineyard in France. He comes out of retirement to investigate a group of Romulan spies, the Borg, and a community of artificial life forms living on a desert planet. Jonathan Frakes and Marina Sirtis appeared on the show playing their *Star Trek: The Next Generation* characters, Will Riker and Deanna Troi. Brent Spiner appeared as both Data and a new character, Alton Soong, the son of Data's creator, Dr. Noonian Soong.

Over ten episodes, *Star Trek: Picard* showed a new side of the retired admiral. He was older and more frail. He could no longer drive a dune buggy. This version of Picard relied on his younger, stronger friends to help get him out of trouble. One thing he still had, however, was his clear and focused mind. Picard could still outwit his enemies and talk his way out of a jam if need be. On occasion, he still commanded the crew to "Engage" or "Make it so."

Fans seemed to like this new Picard. The show scored high ratings and inspired numerous books, comics, and toys. *Star Trek: Picard* was nominated for five Emmy Awards and won one, for Outstanding Prosthetic Makeup. Patrick Stewart also won a Critics Choice Super Award for Best Actor in a Science Fiction/Fantasy Series.

Soon after the series ended in March 2020, producers announced plans for a second season of *Star Trek: Picard*. This time, the retired admiral would be joined by old friend Guinan, played by Whoopi Goldberg, on a new adventure. Many of the cast from season one also agreed to return for more episodes.

Captain and commander, diplomat and action hero, Jean-Luc Picard has fulfilled many roles in Starfleet over the years. He began as a brash young cadet, took the helm of a Federation starship, and currently lives on as a respected elder who is still handy with a phaser—and a sword.

While new adventures are still to be written, his place in the hearts of fans is already secure. Polls consistently rank Picard at the top of the list of favorite *Star Trek* characters. Some think he is the *Enterprise's* greatest captain. When he first appeared on television screens in 1987, he was considered a most unusual hero. But the character eventually became beloved by Trek fans everywhere. Today, it is impossible to imagine *Star Trek* without Picard—or to picture the bridge of the *Enterprise*-D and not see the bald, stern-faced man in the captain's chair leaning forward and, in a most serious voice, giving the order:

"Engage."

Bibliography

Carter, Chip. *Star Trek: The Wisdom of Picard*. New York: Adams Media, 2020.

Goodman, David A. *The Autobiography of Jean-Luc Picard*. London: Titan Books, 2017.

Gross, Edward, and Mark Altman. *Captains' Logs: The Unauthorized Complete Trek Voyages*. New York: Little, Brown and Company, 1995.

Nemecek, Larry. *The Star Trek: The Next Generation Companion*. New York: Pocket Books, 1995.

Ruditis, Paul. *The Star Trek Book: Strange New Worlds Boldly Explained*. New York: DK Publishing, 2016.

Van Hise, James. *Trek: The Next Generation Crew Book*. New York: Pioneer Books, 1993.

Weber, Thomas E., and Emily Joshu, eds. *TIME: Star Trek: Inside the Most Influential Science-Fiction Series Ever*. New York: Meredith Corporation, 2019.

Timeline of Captain Picar

| 2305 | 2323 | 2327 | 2333 | 2364 |

Enters Starfleet
Academy

Graduates from
Starfleet Academy

Takes command of
the *U.S.S. Stargazer*

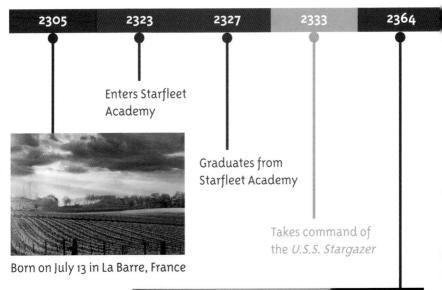

Born on July 13 in La Barre, France

Assumes command of the *U.S.S. Enterprise*-D

d

| 2367 | 2372 | 2381 | 2385 | 2399 |

Promoted to
admiral

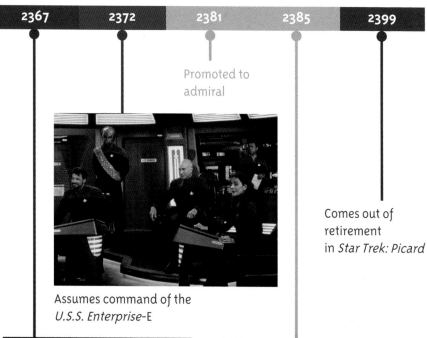

Assumes command of the
U.S.S. Enterprise-E

Comes out of
retirement
in *Star Trek: Picard*

Assimilated by the Borg

Resigns from Starfleet and retires
to Château Picard